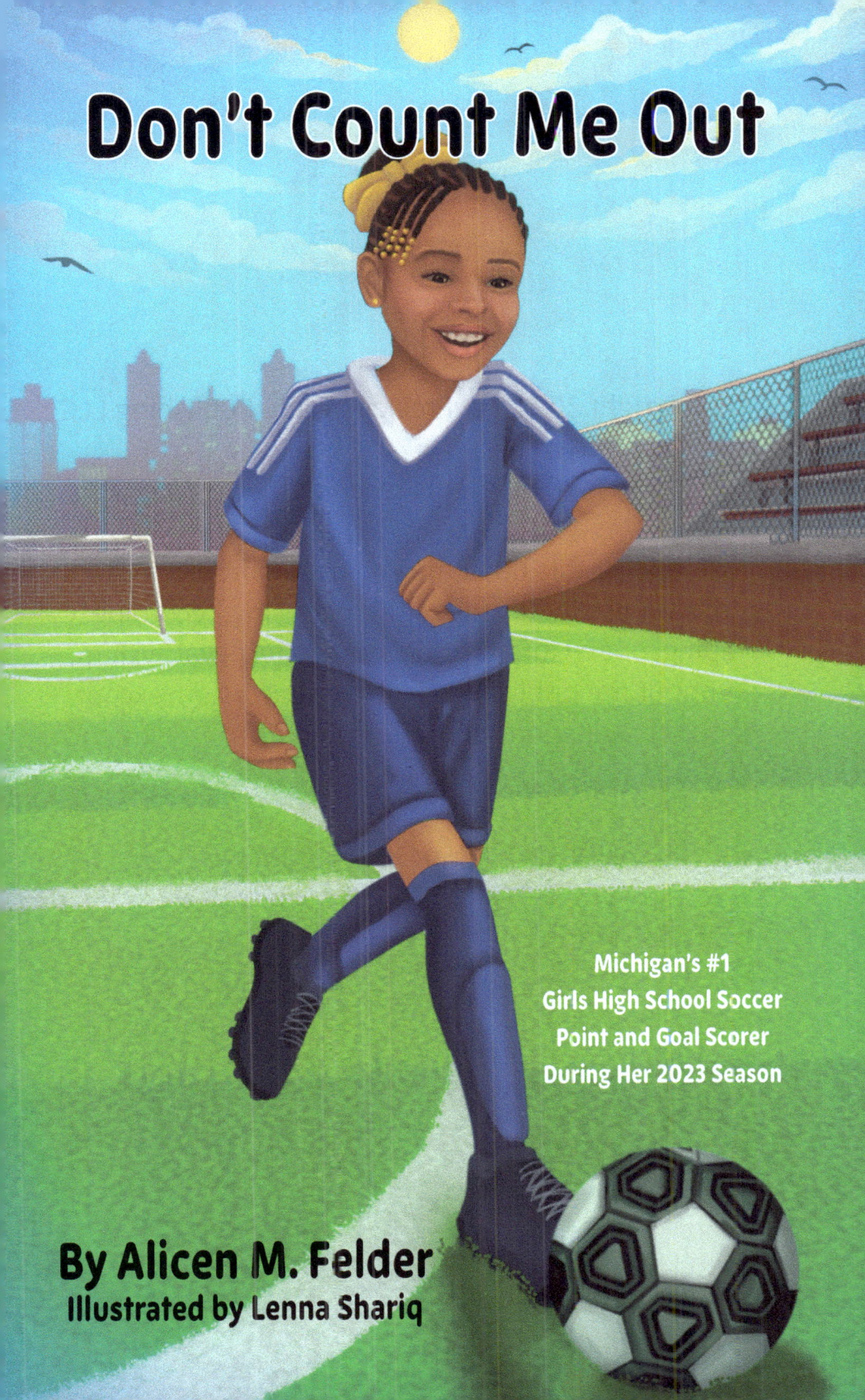

© Copyright 2024, My PreciousApple Publishing LLC

All rights reserved.

No part of this book may be used or reproduced mechanically, including photocopying, recording, taping, or any information storage retrieval system, without the publisher's written permission, except for brief quotations embodied in critical articles and reviews.

ISBN: 978-1-7350450-6-1 (hardcover)
979-8-3202736-6-2 (paperback)

This book is dedicated to kids like me who have big dreams. Never allow anyone to get into your head and tell you what you can't do. You can do anything you put your mind to. You must believe in yourself, work hard, don't quit, and don't let people count you out.

Thank you to my parents, family, friends, and coaches for believing in me and supporting me: Coach Howard, Coach Eddie, Coach Jack, Coach Jim, Coach Addie, and Coach Meyah.

Special thanks to Detroit Public Schools Director of Athletics, MiKyle Covington, for believing in me and encouraging me and other student-athletes. You will never be forgotten.

My name is Alicen, but everyone knows me as Apple, KimMia's little sister. When I was three years old, I fell in love with soccer just from watching my older sister, KimMia, play.

KimMia played soccer with the Rosedale Soccer League, and I enjoyed seeing her practice and play with her teammates. KimMia and her teammates always seemed to be having fun running, chasing the ball, and working together to win games.

I loved the times when my sister would let me practice with her. KimMia would get tired of me asking her to let me play, and when she did, she would kick the ball really far and tell me to go get it. I used to get so tired and sweaty running after the ball, but I did not care. I was having fun being with my big sister and playing soccer, even though I know my mom made her play with me.

KimMia would tell my mom I was too small to play with her. I tried to show my sister that I was a big girl like she was. You see, I thought my sister was the coolest kid ever and that her soccer team had the coolest uniforms. I wanted to be just like her and wear the same soccer uniform too.

I told our mom I wanted to play soccer, but mom said I was too young. She said I could not play in the league until I was 4. To my delight, the following season, when I was four years old, my mom signed me up along with my sister to play for Rosedale.

I screamed with excitement when my mom brought my soccer uniform home. I couldn't wait to put it on. I had not been assigned to a team or had my first practice, but I put my uniform on and practiced all by myself. I practiced as much as possible and tried to do all the moves KimMia and her teammates did.

When the season started, my first coach was Coach Karla, who taught me that soccer is simple. Coach Karla said all players in this sport must use their feet, head, or chest to play the ball. She also said only the goalie can use their hands. Coach let everyone on the team know that the game objective is to score a goal by kicking or heading the ball into the opposing team's net. I let Coach know I was ready and could do all of that. I played every position on the soccer team, but being the goalie was the toughest for me. I admit I would cry a little bit when the opposing team scored when I was the goalie. As time passed, I learned not to cry or get angry but to protect the net better.

The more games I played, the more I realized that soccer was everything I thought it would be and more. I had fun chasing after the ball and wearing my uniform. Everyone thought I was so cute, but I didn't want to just be cute. I wanted to be a great soccer player. Before I knew it, I had completed not one but two soccer seasons. I had played over 24 games, and my game was improving.

By age 6, I had gotten a lot better at soccer. I learned to put the ball in the net and pass the ball around effortlessly. I was kicking, heading, kneeing, and shooting the ball like a pro during my games. I had worked hard during practices and even started practicing with kids older than me. Parents, coaches, and some of my teammates started calling me a beast because other players had a difficult time guarding me and keeping me from scoring. People in the stands often yelled my name, "Apple, Apple, Apple," supporting and encouraging me to continue to play hard.

I loved all my coaches at Rosedale and learned something unique from each one of them through our drills, scrimmages, and games. Coach Karla taught me to have fun, Coach Eddie always reminded me to follow my ball, and Coach Howard always told me to communicate with my teammates on the field. Even today, I still do each of these things in every game I play.

Coach Howard will always be special to me because when I was 7 years old, he allowed me to practice and play with kids 15 and 16 years old. All the older kids counted me out, saying I was tiny and just a baby. They didn't realize I didn't care how small or old I was; I just knew I wanted to play, and I wanted that ball more than anyone else on that field.

Coach Howard allowed me to play in the games with the high school kids when they were short of players or needed a substitute. At first, some of the older kids laughed at me for playing with these big kids who were twice my size, but that was until I got on the field. Whenever I played soccer, I showed up and showed out.

I made those older kids realize that I'm not to be taken as a joke and not to count me out. The more experienced players started to welcome me into games as time passed.

The older I got, the more I learned. I learned more rules and fancy techniques from my coaches and other players. I watched professional soccer games and ate healthier foods. I knew all the soccer positions and language, like center, forward, offsides, corner kicks, throw-in, red card, assist, defender, and many other soccer words. I learned which plays were illegal and would earn teams a flag. I became a walking soccer dictionary. I learned to stay focused and not let anyone or anything take me out of my game.

After years of playing soccer with Rosedale, I met Coach Jim. Coach Jim had a travel league and wanted to recruit me. He asked my parents if I could play for his travel team. Coach Jim said he had been watching my game and felt I could help his team win games. My parents agreed, and in the sixth grade, I joined the Hamburg Soccer League and continued to play with Rosedale during the summer.

Playing for a travel team and some other soccer organizations helped keep me in shape and helped me grow in soccer. While playing with the travel league, I played soccer outside of Detroit and noticed many players did not look like me.

On some teams and in several games, I was the only girl or African American. Some of the opposing teams' parents and players were not nice to me. I was called awful words during some games, and Coach Jim always handled it. He would either end the games or ask the referees to remove the parents calling me mean names. There were also games where players would refuse to shake my hand at the end of games, but I refused to let that bother me. I know soccer is a sport for everyone who wants to play it. Coach told me he'd handle all those situations and that I should play my game.

I was told that in the United States, not many African Americans or females played professional soccer, and hearing that made me want to take action because I loved the game so much. I realized I needed to tell more people who looked like me how fun soccer games are.

I tell everyone you will love soccer if you enjoy running, working as a team, and competing. As a team, my soccer teammates and I run the field and support each other to get the team a win. Soccer has no "I"; we win or lose together, and I love working in a group. I also love soccer because it has given me a second family. My soccer family and I have celebrated birthdays and holidays together, helped one another with school assignments, and regularly check up on each other. We still use group chats to stay updated on what everyone is doing.

Since I was 9 years old, I dreamed of going to Cass Technical High School, and after applying, I was accepted. I was excited to hear Cass had an excellent academic program and soccer team. I knew the school was full of opportunities. I prepared myself for soccer tryouts and made the team. I was ecstatic! I went to all our practices, got to know my teammates, and even had my teammates come to my house for us to bond better. The next thing you know, our first game was here.

I had my #18 green and white soccer uniform and was ready! Cleats, shin guards, and my water bottle. I was starting in the first game. My coaches, Meyah and Jack, gave us our positions, and the next thing I heard was the whistle blown. I'm playing and playing, but the game was not going how I thought it would.

I needed to live up to the name I made for myself and play up to my potential. There was no evidence of the person others called a beast. I was put on the bench for a short time during the game. I was furious at myself for not playing well. I never wanted that to happen again. I changed my mindset, asked my coaches more questions, worked harder at practice, and connected with my teammates more. Soccer is a mental game, so I changed my mentality and returned to playing my original aggressive game.

After that game, I played with high intensity and an open mind. Everything was going well, then I was injured during a play when a player kicked me in the head while going for the ball. I suffered a concussion and had to take time off soccer to get well. I could only practice and play soccer once I recovered. When I did return to soccer towards the end of the season, I was on top of my game.

I received my first "hat trick." I was so excited! A "hat trick" is when a player scores three or more goals, and I did it! My teammates were happy for me too, and we celebrated together. As my game continued to improve, I was recognized as the number 1 scorer and point holder in Michigan for Girls High School Soccer during my season. At the end of the season, I received trophies as the Top Offensive Player and Most Goals Scored from my high school. I was excited to receive a certificate stating that I had earned a varsity soccer patch for a letterman's jacket.

During my second year of high school, things continued to get better. I participated in several tournaments and camps where I met new players and strengthened my game. I was so happy to win the 2024 DPSCD Ally Indoor Player of the Soccer League Award. I know all my awards and trophies resulted from my love for the game, dedication, and hard work.

As I think about the years I have played soccer and my good and bad experiences, I know those experiences were supposed to happen. My mom always says anything someone wants in life will come with challenges.

I learn from all my challenges and welcome every good experience. I understand my good soccer experiences do not happen because I am the best dribbler, have all the moves, or have the best finishing, but because I listen to my coaches, practice, give 110%, and connect with my teammates. So even though I may not be the biggest or the strongest or look the part, I will always work the hardest and make sure nobody counts me out.

Questions

1. Can all soccer players use their hands to play the ball?

2. What did Apple do to improve her soccer game?

3. Some parents and players were mean to Apple while she played with the travel league. How did Coach Jim handle this situation?

4. What caused Apple's concussion?

5. What is a hat trick?

6. Think of a time when people did not believe in you and your ability to do something. How did you prove them wrong?

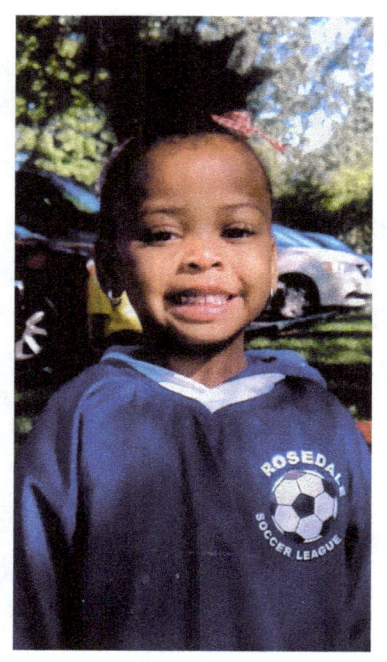

2012

2013

2015

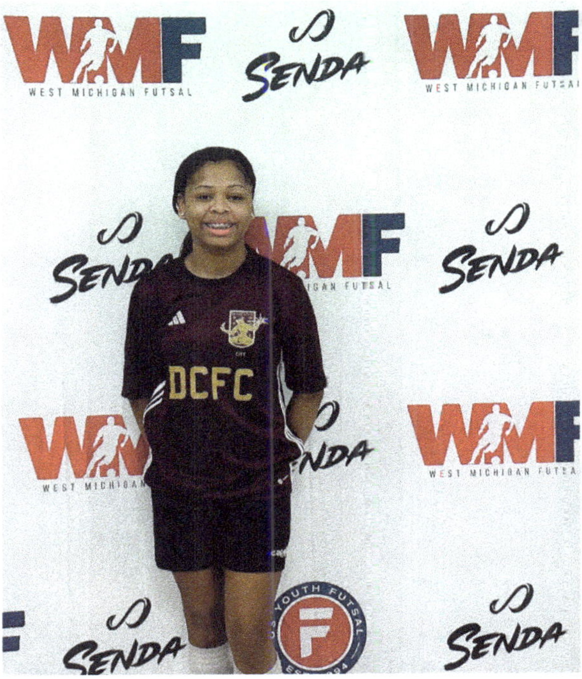

WMF
WEST MICHIGAN FUTSAL
SENDA
DCFC
US YOUTH FUTSAL

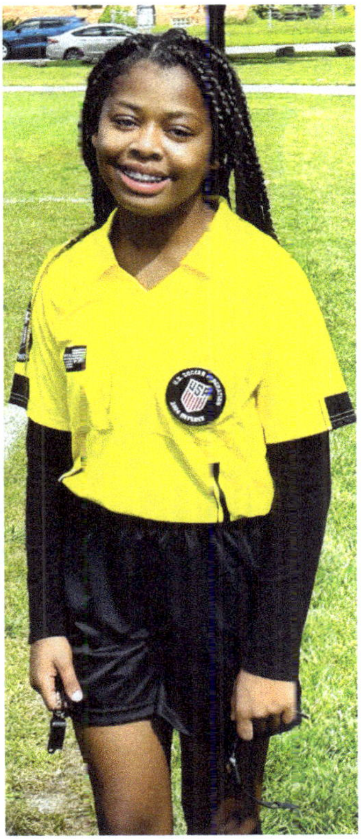

SAGINAW VALLEY
YEO & YEO
PRESENTS
SPIRIT OF SAGINAW
INVITATIONAL
DETROIT CHEVY DEALERS

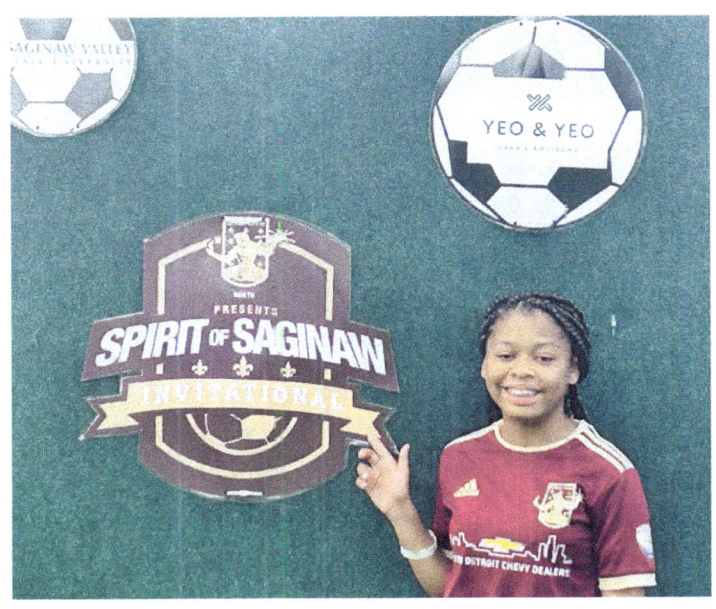

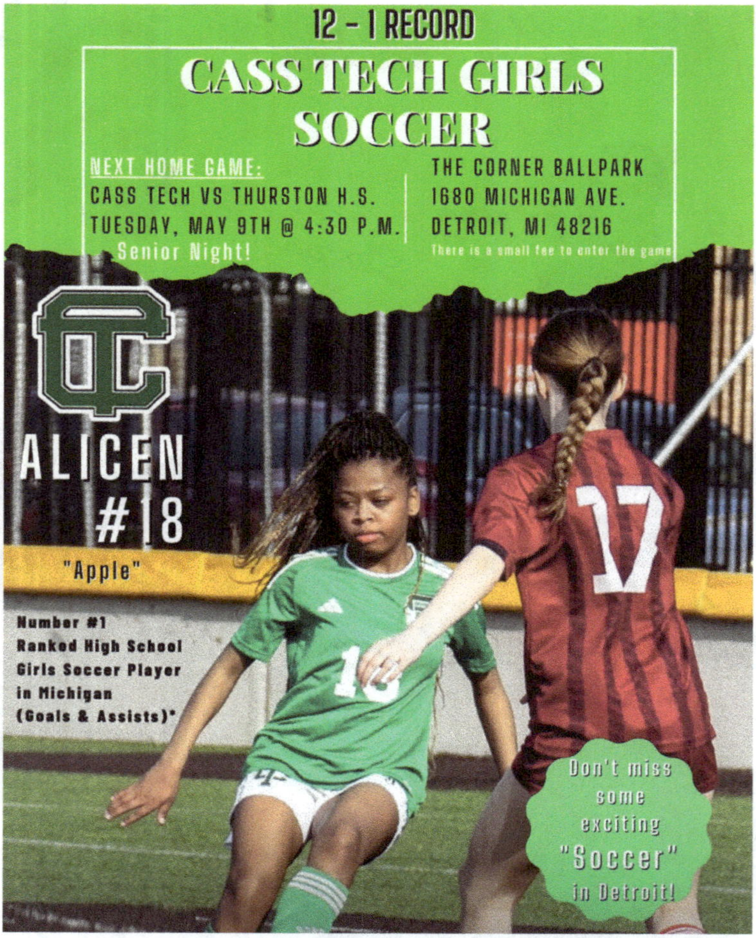
12 - 1 RECORD
CASS TECH GIRLS SOCCER
NEXT HOME GAME:
CASS TECH VS THURSTON H.S.
TUESDAY, MAY 9TH @ 4:30 P.M.
Senior Night!
THE CORNER BALLPARK
1680 MICHIGAN AVE.
DETROIT, MI 48216
There is a small fee to enter the game
ALICEN
#18
"Apple"
Number #1 Ranked High School Girls Soccer Player in Michigan (Goals & Assists)*
Don't miss some exciting "Soccer" in Detroit!

MICHIGAN
STATE YOUTH SOCCER ASSOCIATION
EST. 1976

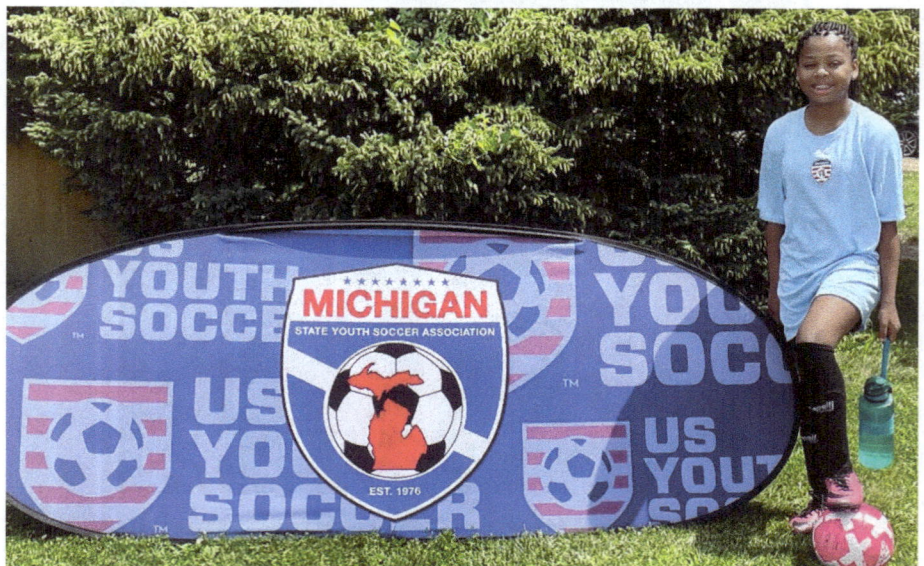

About the Author

Alicen Marie Felder is a 16-year-old writer from Detroit, Michigan. She writes about her life experiences and aims to motivate and inspire all people. In 2020, Alicen published *Say A Little Prayer*, detailing her struggle with speaking and how prayer and work turned things around for her. In her latest book release, *Don't Count Me Out*, Alicen shares her journey of overcoming challenges and becoming  a varsity soccer player at Cass Technical High School, the Detroit Public Schools Community District's 2024 Ally Player of the Girls High School Indoor Soccer Season, and being the #1 Girls High School Soccer Point and Goal Scorer in Michigan during her season.

Alicen enjoys soccer, public speaking, writing, and acting and uses her talents and experiences to inspire and motivate others worldwide.

www.ingramcontent.com/pod-product-compliance
Lightning Source LLC
Chambersburg PA
CBHW072150200426
43209CB00051B/1037